T0082394

THIS BOOK IS FOR:

____

GIVEN IN LOVE FROM:

____

ON THE SPECIAL DAY OF:

____

See what love the Father has given us, that we should be called children of God.
—1 John 3:1

For my dad.
—L.S.

To my nieces, Emma and Eevi.
—S.E.

2024 First Printing
My Tender Heart Devotions

ISBN 978-1-64060-901-3

Library of Congress Control Number 2023058152

10 9 8 7 6 5 4 3 2 1
Cover design: Paraclete Design
Cover image: Sandra Eide

Published by Paraclete Press
Brewster, Massachusetts
www.paracletepress.com

Manufactured by Thomson Press, India. Printed in March 2024.
This product conforms to all applicable CPSIA standards.

Written by **LAURA SASSI**
Illustrated by **SANDRA EIDE**

CONTENTS

HONEY CUBS
PSALM 119:103–104

Buzz, buzz, buzz.
We are busy, busy bees.
Buzz, buzz, buzz.
Sipping nectar as we please.
Clomp, clomp, clomp.
Now, we're bears who want to eat.
Paw, dip, slurp.
Three cubs gobble. What a treat!

How sweet are your words to my taste, sweeter than honey to my mouth!

—Psalm 119:103

STICKY! YUMMY! Bees make honey from the pollen and nectar they get from flowers. The honey is so delicious, bears can't resist it. Maybe you like honey too. King David sure did. We know this because he compared God's Word to honey—full of tasty truth, sweet promises, and wise advice. As King David knew so well, God's Word helps us understand just how much God loves us and that His love is sweet indeed.

HEART MOMENT: Pretend you are bears at a tea party. Drizzle honey on toast. Put it on top of a yogurt parfait or stir it into a cup of tea. As you enjoy the honey goodness, marvel at how good God's Word is too.

BIKE ARMOR
EPHESIANS 6:10–18

I'm all zipped up. My shoes are tied.
My water bottle's by my side.
My helmet's strapped beneath my chin.
Brring, brring. This ride can now begin!

Put on all of God's armor. Then you can remain strong against the devil's evil plans.

—*Ephesians 6:11, NIrV*

SNAP. CLICK. Bike armor keeps you safe when riding. Did you know God also gives us invisible *spiritual* armor or gear for the ride called life? This armor includes things like the belt of truth, the shield of faith, and the helmet of salvation. You can't see or hold God's armor. But it's *like* armor because it helps protect us against the devil's evil ways. And how do we wear God's invisible *spiritual* armor? We wear it by reading and understanding the Bible, by inviting Jesus to be our Savior, and by praying to Him every day.

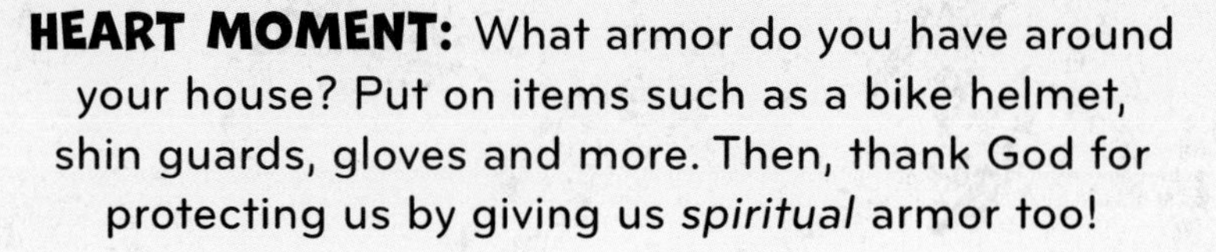

HEART MOMENT: What armor do you have around your house? Put on items such as a bike helmet, shin guards, gloves and more. Then, thank God for protecting us by giving us *spiritual* armor too!

FAMILY RULES
EXODUS 20:12

Mommy says to look both ways
before I cross the street,
and not to grab and reach for food
when we sit down to eat.

Daddy tells me every night
to put my toys away.
It's all because they love me,
so I listen and obey.

Children, obey your parents in everything, for this is your acceptable duty in the Lord.

—*Colossians 3:20*

LOVE, CARE, PROTECT. God has given special grownups in your life an important job—taking care of you! That's a big job, but they do it gladly because they love you so much. Their special job includes loving you, taking care of your daily needs, and teaching you what is good and true and right. How can you love them in return? One way is by listening and obeying. It's like this with God, our heavenly Father, too. He loves it when we listen and obey.

HEART MOMENT: Name some of the ways your parents, or other special guardians, care for you. Then take out paper and crayons and make a card that says, "Thank You for Caring for Me." Draw some of the ways you care for and love each other.

FAWN FAITH
PROVERBS 15:3

See that fawn in the shade?
She looks ready to sleep.
I will count all her spots
but I won't make a peep.

I'll just blow her a kiss
as I gently pass by,
for I know that her mama
is watching nearby.

The LORD will keep your going out and your coming in from this time on and forevermore.

—Psalm 121:8

TIPTOE. HUSH. A baby deer is called a fawn. When first born, a fawn will wobble and need extra rest. If you spot a fawn curled up alone, let it be. Its mama carefully chose that spot so her baby will be safe while she looks for food. But, don't worry. That mama is keeping careful watch. The Bible says God is always keeping watch over you, too. We can have faith. He is always near.

HEART MOMENT: Play "Find the Fawn" with your family. Hide a baby stuffed animal in a cozy spot. See if your loved ones can find it. When they do, whisper, "Hush, there's a fawn on the lawn." After playing, give thanks that like a mama deer who watches over her fawn, God is watching over you!

TOY SAILBOAT
MARK 4:35–41

In the fountain, safe and sound,
tiny boats float all around.
Mine has a sail and sturdy mast.
With my stick, I push it fast!
It's fun until, *drip-drop*, oh no!
A summer storm! Quick—home we go!

And they were filled with great fear and said to one another, "Who then is this, that even the wind and the sea obey him?"

—*Mark 4:41*

SPLASH! BOUNCE! One day Jesus was asleep in a boat when a big storm came. His disciples were scared, so they woke Him. "Save us!" they hollered. Can you guess what Jesus did? He commanded the storm to stop. And it did! Then He reminded His disciples of something very important: They needed to put their faith in Him. Jesus can calm the storms in our lives too. Will you trust Him to quiet the wind and the waves?

HEART MOMENT: Construct a little boat for your tub or pool. Make waves with your hands, then stop and wait for the water to be still again. As you do, give thanks that Jesus is with you through every storm.

ROCKET SHIP
EZEKIEL 36:26

I broke my favorite car today.
It hurtled off the slide.
I didn't think that it would break,
but it burst open wide.

I put it back together,
but in a brand-new way.
Now it is a rocket ship
all set to blast away!

So if anyone is in Christ, there is a new creation: everything old has passed away; look, new things have come into being!

—2 Corinthians 5:17

OLD. NEW! God is the master of taking old things and making them brand new. He doesn't do it with toy cars. Instead, the Bible says He transforms *us*! When we ask Jesus to be the master of our hearts, God takes all our brokenness and sin and makes us new. What's our job? We need to admit that we need Jesus and His gift of forgiveness, then ask Him to be the master of our hearts.

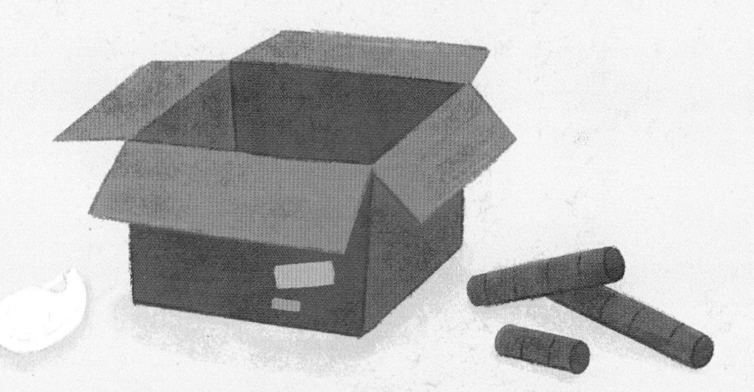

HEART MOMENT: Find some cardboard boxes or paper towel rolls and craft something new. As you transform the old into something even better, give thanks that this is what Jesus does with us when we believe and trust in Him.

THIRSTY PUPPY

JOHN 4:7–15

My puppy has a water bowl.
I keep it on a tray.
It sits there in the kitchen
while we run and romp and play.

And after all that fetch and fun,
I bring it to the sink.
With wagging tail, my puppy waits,
then—*splash*—it takes a drink!

"Those who drink of the water that I will give them will never be thirsty."

—*John 4:14*

LAP. GULP. Puppy dogs and people get thirsty. One day Jesus was thirsty, so He asked a woman for water. As she pulled a full bucket from the well, Jesus said He could give her something called *living* water and she'd never be thirsty again. She wanted some! Jesus wasn't talking about ordinary water. He was talking about *spiritual* water. If we seek Him, we will never be spiritually thirsty again, because God nourishes us as we are filled with His Spirit.

HEART MOMENT: Pour yourself a cold glass of water. As you drink, give thanks that Jesus is our Living Water and that He loves it when we are thirsty for Him.

BUNNY EARS

MARK 4:23

My sweet little bunny,
some think you look funny
with ears poking up in the air.

But those ears come in handy,
and *I* think they're dandy
for listening to sounds everywhere.

Then from the cloud came a voice that said, "This is my Son, my Chosen; listen to him!"

—Luke 9:35

HUSH. LISTEN. Long, tall ears help rabbits hear even the smallest sound. This super ability allows rabbits to respond quickly to any situation. Like bunnies, God wants us to use our ears to listen and respond to His teachings. But who should we be listening to? God spells it right out: HIS SON! And who is that? JESUS!

HEART MOMENT: Get very quiet. Then, like a bunny, listen carefully. What kinds of sounds do you hear? Can you name at least five different sounds? Thank God for giving you ears to listen and learn about Him at home and at church.

CLOCK TRUST
ECCLESIASTES 3:1–8

Tick-tock, I love
how Grandpa's clock
tick-tocks throughout the day.

To let me know
just when—*tick-tock*—
to wake or eat or play!

I trust in you, O Lord; I say, "You are my God." My times are in your hand.

—*Psalm 31:14–15*

WHIR-GONG! What kinds of things fill your time? Most likely, some are happy things like going to a birthday party. Some are sad things like when you are sick. The Bible says there is a time for everything. But here is some very good news: Whatever the time, early or late, happy or sad, you can trust God is with you all the time and that He loves you very much.

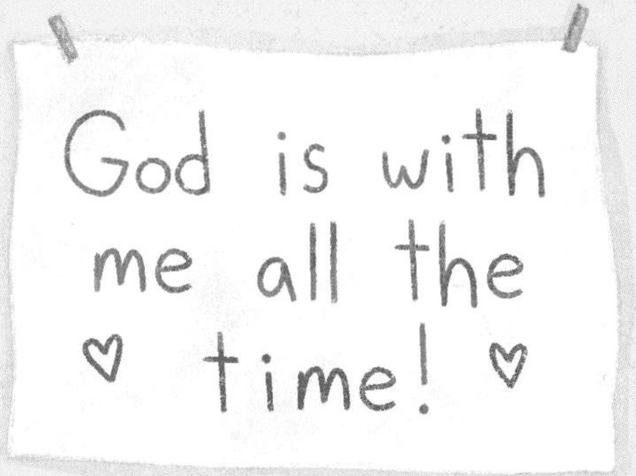

God is with
me all the
time!

HEART MOMENT: Go on a hunt for all the clocks in your house. Then, on a large piece of paper, write, "God is with me all the time!" Fill the page, naming or drawing all the ways you spend your time. Hang it as a reminder of God's loving presence—night and day.

LUNCH PLAN
JOHN 6:5–14

I like to cut my sandwich
into chunky little squares,
served with crunchy carrot sticks
or juicy cut-up pears.

Packed snuggly in my lunch box,
it can travel anywhere.
And if my friend forgets *her* lunch,
it's easy now to share!

"There is a boy here who has five barley loaves and two fish."

—*John 6:9*

PICNIC TIME! As Jesus was teaching, a huge crowd gathered. Jesus wanted to feed them lunch. "There are too many people," his disciples said. "It would cost too much." Then a boy gave Jesus his lunch. It was very small—just five barley loaves and two small fish. Jesus blessed the food and passed it around. It was a picnic miracle! Five thousand people were fed, with twelve baskets full of leftovers! Jesus's followers learned that God can use even the smallest offering to bless others in big ways.

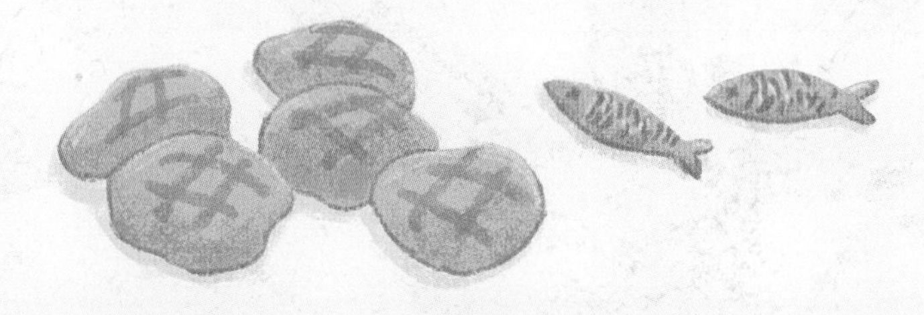

HEART MOMENT: Make a "loaves and fishes" list of small things you can do for others this week to share God's love. Then, thank Jesus for using even our smallest offerings to serve others in big ways.

PRECIOUS COIN

LUKE 15:8–10

Today I lost my precious coin.
I heard it bounce and roll.
And that's how I discovered
that my pocket had a hole.

My coin was small and silver
with a shiny tail and head.
I looked until I found it.
It had rolled beneath my bed!

"Rejoice with me, for I have found the coin that I had lost."

—Luke 15:9

WOBBLE. PLINK! Jesus once told the story of a woman who lost a coin. She was very upset and cleaned her whole house looking for it. And how did she feel when she found it? She had a party and rejoiced! Jesus searches and looks for each of us. And how does Jesus respond when we are found? Jesus says He and God and the angels celebrate with great joy!

HEART MOMENT: Gather coins, thin paper, and a crayon. Place the coins under the paper. Using the peeled side of the crayon, rub firmly across the paper. The imprint of the coins should appear. Hang your coin rubbing in a special spot as a reminder that Jesus rejoices when He finds us.

JOYFUL NOISES
PSALM 66:1–4

Clapping, tapping, plucking strings,
jingling our tambourines.
Blowing horns and striking gongs,
singing loud our joyful songs.
I love how we each have a part.
I praise You, God, with all my heart.

Make a joyful noise to God, all the earth.

—Psalm 66:1

JINGLE! STRUM! God loves it when we praise Him with joyful noises. To praise means to lift our hearts and souls and give our *all* to God, thanking Him for all He has done and all He is. A joyful way to do this is by singing songs of praise with instruments and voices and our whole beings! Can you think of a time you have praised God?

HEART MOMENT: Name some of the wonderful things God has done. Then praise God with a song or a melody played on the instrument of your choice. Whatever you choose, praise Him with all your heart.

MY ROCK
MATTHEW 7:24–27

There's a rock I like to visit
when I am by the lake.
It's big and round and solid.
It doesn't move or shake.

Through every storm and season,
it has stood the test of time.
It's sturdy, indestructible,
and made for me to climb!

"Everyone, then, who hears these words of mine and acts on them will be like a wise man who built his house on rock."

—*Matthew 7:24*

HAMMER! THUNK! Jesus once told a story about two men who were building houses. One man chose to build on sand. The other chose solid rock. Jesus explained that the rock was like God's Word—strong and dependable. When a big storm came, the house on the sand fell down, but the house on the rock stood strong. It's like that with God too. If we build our life according to what the Bible says, nothing can wash away our faith.

HEART MOMENT: Draw a picture of a house built on a rock, then hang it by your bed to remind you that God and His Word are like rocks. We can depend on them!

SPRING NEST

LUKE 24:1–5

In a nest of leaves and thatch,
it's time for springtime chicks to hatch.
I hear and watch them *tap-tap-tap*
until, at last, their shells go *CRACK!*
Cheep! Cheep! The tiny birds are sweet.
And now, it seems, it's time to eat.

In his great mercy he has given us a new birth and a living hope. This hope is living because Jesus Christ rose from the dead.

—1 Peter 1:3, NIrV

CHEEP, CHEEP. Have you ever seen a nest filled with eggs? What hatches out of those eggs? Precious chicks! These fluffy new hatchlings are a wonderful reminder of God's love. Jesus didn't break out of a shell, but on Easter morning, He broke out of the cold, hard tomb when He rose again! When we open our hearts to Jesus, the Bible says we are given new hope and life through the gift of Jesus's death and resurrection.

HEART MOMENT: Gather some plastic eggs. Then, using yarn wrapped into pom-poms, create little chicks to go in each shell. Hide the eggs and take turns finding them. Like chicks that hatch from their shells, rejoice that we can enjoy new birth through Jesus.

ONE TINY SEED
MATTHEW 17:14–16, 19–20

One tiny seed tucked in the ground
and watered every day,
with lots of sun and tender care,
sprouts in a wondrous way.

First stem and leaves reach for the sky
with mighty growing power,
until, at last, one sunny day
out bursts a joyous flower!

"For truly I tell you, if you have faith the size of a mustard seed...nothing will be impossible for you."
—*Matthew 17:20*

SEED, SOIL, SUN. One day Jesus's disciples were having trouble performing a miracle. "Why are we having such a hard time?" they asked. Jesus showed them a little seed and explained it was a matter of faith. Faith is trusting in God even when things seem impossible. All the disciples needed was faith the size of a tiny seed. Jesus put it this way: "If you have faith the size of a mustard seed...nothing will be impossible for you!" Do you have faith the size of a seed?

HEART MOMENT: Plant a tiny seed in soil. Give it daily sunshine and water. Wait for it to sprout. As it grows a little bigger every day, thank God that He doesn't ask us to have giant faith. All we need is faith as tiny as a seed, and God will do great things—through us and for us!

BABY FOOD
HEBREWS 5:12–14

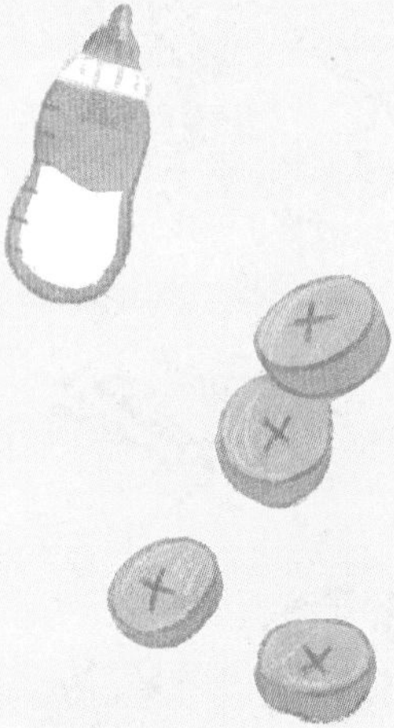

First milk from a bottle,
then spinach purée,
then mushy bananas
on face, hands, and tray!

I guess babies like that,
but that's not my tune.
I prefer big kid meals
with a plate, fork, and spoon!

Anyone who lives on milk is still a baby. That person does not want to learn about living a godly life. Solid food is for those who are grown up.

—Hebrews 5:13–14, NIrV

GURGLE! COO! When you were a baby, you drank milk. Next came wet cereal and lots of messy, goopy things. As you grew, you started eating big kid food and using big kid tools like a plate, fork, and spoon. Growing as God's child is like this too. At first our understanding is simple. But, as we grow and feed on God's Word, our understanding grows. Do you feed on God's Word every day so that you can grow into a big kid for God?

HEART MOMENT: Plan a "big kid" meal for you and your family. Set the table with plates, napkins, and utensils. Then serve up the food. As you eat, give thanks that God has given us the Bible to feed on so we can grow in our understanding of Him.

ALL CLEAN
PSALM 51:1–2

Muddy fingers, muddy toes.
Muddy sneakers, muddy clothes.
Time to wash them double-quick.
Soap and water do the trick.
The mud is gone. The stains are too.
Your clothes are clean—and so are you!

If we confess our sins, he who is faithful and just will forgive us our sins and cleanse us from all unrighteousness.

—1 John 1:9

SPLAT! SMUDGE! Just as our outsides get dirty, our inside heart and soul get muddy too. This happens when we do things we know are wrong. The Bible calls this sin. Sin makes our insides feel awful because it separates us from God, who is holy and clean. This makes God sad, too, so He sent Jesus to cleanse us by giving His life for us on the cross. What's our job? We need to turn from our wrong choices, say we are sorry, and ask for God's forgiveness. Then we can be glad in the fresh, clean start Jesus gives us each day.

HEART MOMENT: Name some ways you have gotten muddy on the inside. Confess those sins to God. Then be happy that through Jesus you are clean!

THE WIND
ISAIAH 41:10

Whoosh! I cannot see the wind,
but it likes to mess my hair.
It sends my bubbles bouncing
and blows petals everywhere!

Its presence is invisible.
as it brushes past my face
—over, under, round about—
filling every space.

"Be strong and courageous; do not be frightened or dismayed, for the LORD your God is with you wherever you go."

—*Joshua 1:9*

RUSTLE, SWISH. We can't see the wind, but we feel it blow. And we see how it moves things—like leaves or bubbles. God is like that too. We can't see Him, but if we open our hearts we will feel His Spirit and we will see His movement in the amazing ways He cares for us and all creation. How do we know for sure that God is always with us? It says so in the Bible!

HEART MOMENT: Find some bubble solution and a wand, then head outside. Stand for a moment and notice the wind. Is it tickling your face? Is it moving any leaves? Then blow your bubbles and see where they go. As you do, give thanks that like invisible wind, God is with you always.

SUNSET HUG
EPHESIANS 4:31–32

The sun is setting on the hill,
but I am very grumpy still.
I'm mad because my puppy dog
slobber-chewed my brand-new clog.

Now it's ruined, but *whimper-tug*,
she's sorry and she wants a hug.
"Okay," I say, "I love you, too,
but next time, please, don't chew my shoe!"

Do not let the sun go down on your anger.
—*Ephesians 4:26*

WHIMPER, TUG. Forgiveness is choosing love over anger when someone does you wrong—like a puppy chewing your favorite shoe! Forgiving others can be hard, but God wants us to forgive just as He forgives us. The Bible has a lot to say about forgiving and living well with others. Why does God want us to let go of anger and forgive, especially before bedtime? Maybe because it's easier to sleep when we make things right with others.

HEART MOMENT: Are you angry with someone about something? Or maybe you are the one who needs to say "I'm sorry"? Will you choose love over anger before the sun sets? Hint: That might mean giving someone a hug to let them know you are sorry or that you forgive them.

SHINY RACE CAR

LEVITICUS 19:11

I found a shiny race car lying on the ground.
No one saw me find it. No one was around.
Then I saw a notice pinned up to a tree.
"LOST: A shiny race car. If found return to me!"
I wanted so to keep it, but a voice inside me said,
"That would be dishonest!" so I gave it back instead.

"Do to others as you would have them do to you."
—*Luke 6:31*

VROOM, VROOM. If someone found your favorite toy, would you want them to pretend it was theirs and take it? No! That's stealing and it's wrong. "You shall not steal," the Bible says. Instead, Jesus shows us the better way: "Do to others as you would have them do to you." This is known as the Golden Rule. Next time you are tempted to be selfish, give yourself the Golden Rule test. If the answer is "I wouldn't want someone to do that to me," then don't do it.

HEART MOMENT: Create a Golden Rule sign on a piece of paper, then decorate it with gold star stickers. Hang it by your bed to help you remember that God wants us to treat others as we want to be treated.

FOGGY PATH
PSALM 25:4–5

In the fog it's hard to see
the path that lies in front of me.
But, then it lifts its milky veil
and I can see the winding trail.

Make me to know your ways, O LORD; teach me your paths.

—Psalm 25:4

UP? DOWN? Sometimes we aren't sure where God's path is leading us. It's as if we are walking in fog. But God is good. He can see through even the thickest fog, and, if you ask Him, He will show you the way. He does this through His Word, the Bible. God also uses special people—like your parents and teachers—to help you see more clearly where to go and what to do. When your path seems foggy, remember we can ask and trust God and the special people He places in our lives to show us the way.

HEART MOMENT: Next time you take a bath or shower, notice how the mirror gets foggy with steam. Take your finger and make a path across the mirror. Then, thank God for giving us the Bible and special people to show us the way, even when everything seems foggy.

RUNNING THE RACE

2 TIMOTHY 4:7–8

We're standing at the starting line
with sneakers laced up tight.
The whistle blows. It's time to go!
We run with all our might.

And when we reach the finish line,
we hear the coaches say,
"Good job! You made it to the end.
You did your best today!"

And let us keep on running the race marked out for us. Let us keep looking to Jesus.

—Hebrews 12:1–2, NIrV

READY, SET, GO! Do you like to run? It's hard work and you feel breathless at the end, but how good it feels to cross the finish line! In the Bible, our life with Jesus is compared to a race. Jesus is both beside us and at the finish line waiting for us. And all along the way, special people are cheering for us. Are you ready to put on your spiritual sneakers and run the race for Jesus?

HEART MOMENT: Create your own race course. Then run some races. As you cheer each other on, remember that in the race called life, Jesus is right there beside you, helping you every step of the way. Will you ask Him to be your Coach and Savior?

SWEET BLESSINGS

PSALM 100:5

Gingerbread, lemon tarts,
cookies and cake.
Oh, how my grandma
and I love to bake.

And when she is with me,
or when she's away,
the love that we share
is a nibble away!

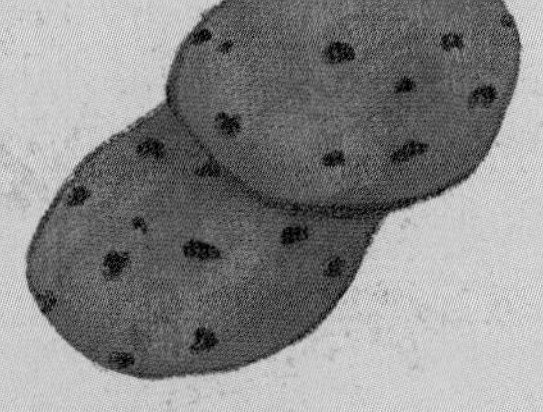

O taste and see that the LORD is good.

—*Psalm 34:8*

MMMM. GOOD. Do you have a favorite dessert? God doesn't bake cookies or cakes, but He sure knows how to shower us with sweet blessings. King David often praised God for the blessings God sent his way and wrote them down as songs, or psalms. David's blessings included safe shelter, good food, forgiveness, and God's love! God also blesses us in countless ways far sweeter than cookies or cake.

HEART MOMENT: Invite someone to bake with you. Share with one another ways God has blessed you with His love. As you enjoy your sweet treats, thank God for all He has done.

NATURE WALK

PSALM 104:24–25

I see spiders spinning webs
so dainty yet so strong.
Birds and crickets chirp and sing
each with a different song.
I see branches bend and sway.
Moon and sun shine night and day.
As I walk I can't stop praising—
God's creation is amazing!

Ever since the creation of the world God's eternal power and divine nature, invisible though they are, have been seen and understood through the things God has made.

—Romans 1:20

LOOK. MARVEL. Have you ever noticed the amazing detail in a spider web or a snowflake? Or marveled at how God designed trees with branches that burst with leaves? Nature is amazing in both detail and design. All made by God, each leaf, animal, star (and more!) reminds us that God cares about the details of everything—including you! How can we show our appreciation for God and His wonderful creation? One way is by keeping the nature around us clean and well cared for. We can also thank God for giving us all those clues in nature that remind us of Him!

HEART MOMENT: Go on a nature walk. Along the way, stop to marvel at and notice all the wonderful details of a leaf, or a flower, or even a stick. Thank God for being the loving creator of it all. (And if you see some trash, help keep God's creation clean by picking it up and throwing it away.)

MY BASKET
JOSHUA 4:1–8

I have a sturdy basket that
I use when I explore.
I fill it up with special things
like pebbles, sticks, and more.

And when I get back home again,
it's my joy and pleasure
to tip it out so I can tell
the story of each treasure.

"When your children ask in time to come, 'What do those stones mean to you?' then you shall tell them..."

—*Joshua 4:6–7*

PLINK. CLINK. Did you know God asked His chosen people to collect rocks? This happened as they were traveling to God's Promised Land. The Jordan River blocked their way, but God amazingly parted the waters so the people and their animals could cross! As they walked on dry ground, God told their leader, Joshua, to have twelve men collect twelve rocks from the river and stack them in the Promised Land. Why? So when their children saw the rocks, they could tell the story of God's miracle and goodness.

HEART MOMENT: Have everyone in your family choose something from around the house that reminds them of God's goodness. Then have a show-and-tell time. Share the story of your special object.

SALT

COLOSSIANS 4:5–6

Shake, shake—
a little bit of salt,
sprinkled with great care,
turns ordinary French fries
into *frites extraordinaires!*

Let your speech always be gracious, seasoned with salt, so that you may know how you ought to answer everyone.
—*Colossians 4:6*

SPRINKLE, SHAKE. A little salt adds good flavor to food like French fries, pretzels, and popcorn. The way we speak also has the power to add good to the lives of people around us. That's why, as Scripture says, we should do our best to "sprinkle" our words, not with salt, but with grace and love so they point others to the hope we have in Jesus.

HEART MOMENT: At mealtime, pass the saltshaker around. Instead of shaking salt on your food, hold it and shake some words of kindness and grace to each person at the table.

CLIMBING TREE
LUKE 19:1–10

My climbing tree has branches
and though it's not too tall,
when I climb it I can see
the world beyond our wall.

Past the hedges and the walk
straight to the the spot where—*whee!*
I see my friend who also climbs.
She's waving back at me!

So he ran ahead and climbed a sycamore tree to see him, because he was going to pass that way.

—*Luke 19:4*

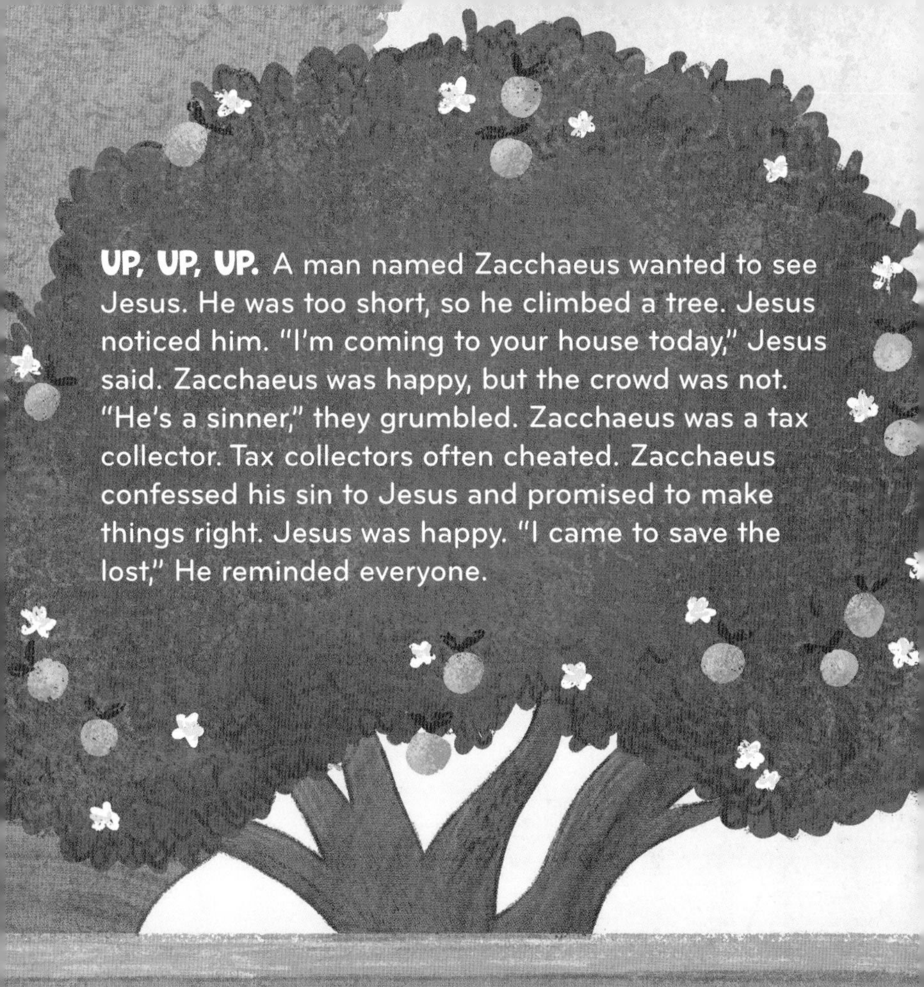

UP, UP, UP. A man named Zacchaeus wanted to see Jesus. He was too short, so he climbed a tree. Jesus noticed him. "I'm coming to your house today," Jesus said. Zacchaeus was happy, but the crowd was not. "He's a sinner," they grumbled. Zacchaeus was a tax collector. Tax collectors often cheated. Zacchaeus confessed his sin to Jesus and promised to make things right. Jesus was happy. "I came to save the lost," He reminded everyone.

HEART MOMENT: With permission, climb something. What can you see from up there? As you look around, remember Jesus loves when, like Zacchaeus, we earnestly seek Him, turn from our wrong choices, and follow Him!

FRUIT SALAD
GALATIANS 5:22–26

Yellow, orange,
green and blue,
with a dash of red tones, too.
Cut in chunks both big and small,
fruit salad is a treat for all!

The fruit of the Spirit is love, joy, peace, patience, kindness, generosity, faithfulness, gentleness, and self-control.

—*Galatians 5:22–23*

CHUNK. SQUIRT. Can you name these fruits? On their own, each fruit is delicious, but in a bowl of salad they're *extra* good. We are kind of like bowls. What does God want to fill us with? Fruit! Not just strawberries or grapes, but spiritual fruit that comes from letting God's Holy Spirit guide our actions. Spiritual fruit nourishes our souls and blesses everyone around us. It includes things like love, joy, gentleness, and more.

HEART MOMENT: Choose several colorful fruits, grab a bowl, and make a fruit salad. As you serve and enjoy your treat, name all the fruit of the Spirit. Thank God for filling us with His fruit!

MY LANTERN
MATTHEW 5:14–16

I have a little lantern
with holes punched out of tin.
It's like a beacon on our porch
glowing from within.

"In the same way, let your light shine before others, so that they may see your good works and give glory to your Father in heaven."

—*Matthew 5:16*

TWINKLE, GLOW. A lantern glowing on the porch fills the darkness and makes visitors want to stop by. We're not lanterns, but did you know Jesus wants us to glow for Him? This is how He puts it: Is a lamp supposed to be covered? No! It's supposed to give light to all the house! Likewise, Jesus wants us to glow for Him by doing good works and pointing others to God. Will you be His shining light?

HEART MOMENT: Make a lantern by painting or covering the outside of a jar in tissue paper. With adult supervision, gently place a candle inside. As it glows, talk about ways you can shine for Jesus!

THUNDERCLAP

JOB 37:2–12

Zip! Zing! When lightning crashes down
and thunder fills the air,
I snuggle under cozy quilts
and say a special prayer.

For God controls the thunderclaps,
the lightning, and the rain.
I can trust the storm will pass
and sun will shine again.

God thunders wondrously with his voice; he does great things that we cannot comprehend.

—*Job 37:5*

CRACK. BOOM. God is the creator of everything, including stormy weather! He is the one who causes the rain to fall, the wind to blow, and the lightning to crack. In the Bible, God's voice is even described as sounding like thunder. So when you hear thunder during a storm, instead of being scared, think of that loud boom as a noisy reminder: God is near and He is in control.

HEART MOMENT: Next time there is a thunderstorm, find a cozy, safe place. Then, with each boom of thunder, imagine what God might be saying to let you know He is with you in the storm.

RAINBOW PROMISE

GENESIS 9:8–17

Can you see that rainbow
like a banner in the sky,
arching over everything
with colors flying high?

It's a bright reminder
of God's promise to restore
a second chance for all to have
full life with Him once more!

"I have set my bow in the clouds, and it shall be a sign of the covenant between me and the earth."

—*Genesis 9:13*

SHIMMER. SHINE. With great love, God created you. Sadly, the first people God created forgot about His love. They turned away and did evil things, so God decided to start over. Only a man named Noah still loved and listened to God. So, when God asked Noah to build an ark and fill it with animals, Noah obeyed. Then God sent a flood that washed everything away except the ark. Noah, his family, and all the animals in the ark floated on top of the waters. Life started over. God promised never again to flood the whole Earth. And what did God put in the sky as a reminder of His promise? A rainbow!

HEART MOMENT: After it rains, look out your window or take a walk to see if you can spot God's rainbow. When you see it, thank God for keeping His promises.

MAGNIFYING GLASS
PSALM 34:2–3

Every little tiny thing,
like seeds and bugs and grass,
suddenly looks *giant*
through this magnifying glass!

O magnify the Lord with me, and let us exalt his name together.

—*Psalm 34:3*

PEEK, LOOK. Have you ever looked through a magnifying glass? Suddenly, a tiny ant has six giant legs and you can see every detail of a tiny seed! It's so amazing that you want to tell everyone about it. When we praise God and tell others about Him, the Bible says we magnify His name. We aren't using magnifying glasses. We aren't making God bigger. He's already bigger than anything in all creation. But when we make a big deal of the ways God is good and how much He loves us, we are magnifying His name so that all will know about our great God!

HEART MOMENT: Use a magnifying glass to explore around your house or outside. As you look through the glass and see little things get big, remember God loves it when we magnify His name. Will you magnify God's name today?

PRECIOUS KITTEN
EPHESIANS 1:3–6

Hello, precious kitten,
so fluffy and brand new.
We heard you need a family
and so we welcome you!

He destined us for adoption as his children through Jesus Christ, according to the good pleasure of his will.
—*Ephesians 1:5*

MEOW. PURR. Has your family or someone you know ever adopted a pet? To adopt means to raise as one's own. Adopted pets quickly become part of the family. We love them and provide everything they need to live well. In a similar way, the Bible says we are adopted into God's family when we accept the saving grace of Jesus. This means we become God's precious children!

HEART MOMENT: Draw or paint a portrait of your family, including any pets. Then hang it somewhere special to help you remember that God wants you to be a part of His family too.

SHINING LOVE
PSALM 18:28

I love to hold my flashlight
and point it in the night.
It makes the path less scary
and the way ahead shine bright.

"I am the light of the world. Whoever follows me will never walk in darkness but will have the light of life."
—*John 8:12*

BLINK! SHINE! Did you know Jesus calls Himself the Light of the World? He doesn't need a battery or a bulb. You can't turn Him on or off by pressing a button. Jesus is *like* a light pointing us to Him. Just as a flashlight (or a torch) makes the dark less scary, Jesus comforts us when we are afraid. He shines His love on us when we feel alone, and He shows us where to go. Will you let Jesus be the light of your life?

HEART MOMENT: Grab a flashlight. When it's dark press the "on" button. Instead of being scared, have fun exploring the dark corners of your room and closet. Then point the light to your cozy bed and crawl on top. As you do, remember that Jesus's love shines bright day or night. He is the light of the world!

QUIET HANDS

MARK 6:45–46

With busy hands I draw and sew.
I stack and build and catch and throw.
But when it's time for me to pray,
I fold my hands a *quiet* way.
Then still and focused, I can start
to talk to God with all my heart.

"Be still, and know that I am God!"

—*Psalm 46:10*

HUSH. FOLD. You can pray to God anywhere and anytime. You can pray when you're running or drawing, at home or at school. But, sometimes it helps to slow down and focus your thoughts by folding your hands and being still. Then you can turn all your attention to God who *loves* when we talk to Him like this. It shows that we can be quiet and want Him to be a part of our lives.

HEART MOMENT: Today, when it is time to pray, take a moment to quiet your hands. Fold them together in prayer, close your eyes, and bow your head. When your heart is still, lift your prayer to Him.

BOOK NOOK
2 KINGS 22:1–23:3

Instead of scattered all around
where some get lost and never found,
I have a basket where I keep
the books I read before I sleep.
Then, when it's time to read a book,
they're all there in my cozy nook.

The king had all the words of the Book of the Covenant read to them. The book had been found in the LORD's temple.

—2 Kings 23:2, NIrV

LOST AND FOUND! King David and King Solomon loved to read God's Word. It helped them know what to do and how to serve God. But after these two kings died, God's Word was lost for many years until King Josiah's priest finally found it. When King Josiah read it, he cried because he realized everyone had forgotten what God's Word said. King Josiah gathered all the people together and read it to them. After hearing the words read, everyone promised with heart and soul to live according to God's Word again.

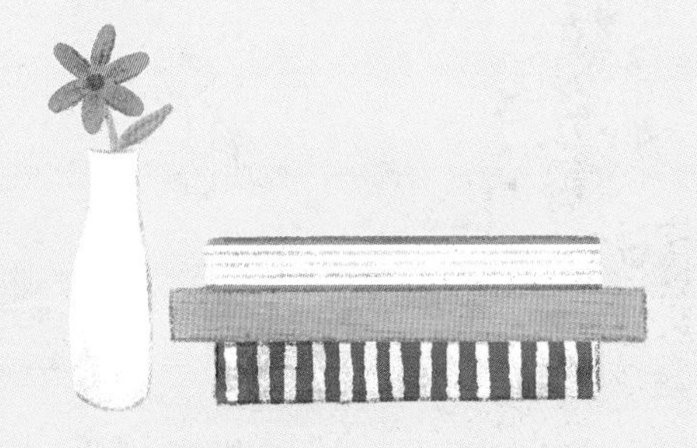

HEART MOMENT: Go on a hunt for all the Bibles around your house. Then pick a special place to keep them so they are easy to find. Plan to read God's Word every day.

CARROT STRENGTH

EPHESIANS 3:16–17

When gentle breezes rustle leaves
and cause long stems to sway,
I'm thankful that these carrot tops
don't bounce and blow away.

I know, *crunch, crunch,* they stay because
beneath each leafy crown,
there is a strong and tasty root
that keeps them anchored down.

You received Christ Jesus as Lord. So keep on living your lives in him. Have your roots in him. Build yourselves up in him.

—Colossians 2:6–7, NIrV

CRUNCH, CRUNCH. Did you know the orange part of a carrot is the root? It holds the plant in place when it is growing so it doesn't blow away. The root also absorbs water and nutrients from the dirt so the carrot plant thrives and grows. God wants us to thrive and grow, too. We aren't rooted in dirt. The Bible says when we accept Jesus, we become rooted in Him. We are rooted in Jesus when we put our trust in Him and find nourishment by reading the Bible and following His teachings.

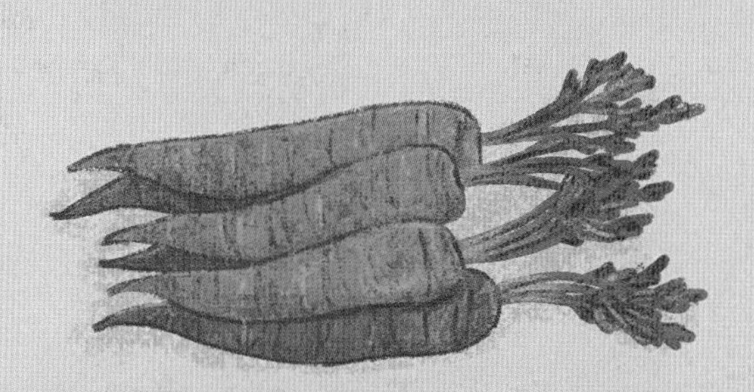

HEART MOMENT: In your garden or at the store, look for carrots that still have green leafy stems. Measure and investigate each carrot in the bunch. Next time you nibble on that crunchy, orange root, give thanks that Jesus invites us to be rooted in Him.

COUNTING HAIRS

PSALM 139:13–16

Black or red or blond or brown,
right side up or upside down,
curly, frizzy, wavy, straight,
the hair we grow is really great.

But when I try to count each hair
to see how much I have up there,
I have so many, I cannot.
Let's just say I have *a lot!*

"And even the hairs of your head are all counted."
—*Matthew 10:30*

SWISH, SWOOSH, CURL. Before you were born, God planned every detail. He created each hair, freckle, and body part you have with love and purpose. God is perfect, which means He doesn't make mistakes. He knows everything about you, and He loves you. As Jesus told His disciples one day, you need never be afraid because you are precious to God. How precious? So precious that He even knows how many hairs are on your head!

HEART MOMENT: Gather brushes and combs, maybe even head bands and barrettes. Then set up a hair station and brush each other's hair. Give one another silly or fancy hairdos. (No scissors allowed.) As you marvel over your new hair styles, give thanks that God loves every detail of you—including your hair!

HUNGRY SQUIRREL
PROVERBS 2:1–8

Little squirrel, I see you there,
grabbing acorns everywhere.
You store them neatly underground,
nice and hidden, safe and sound.
Then comes a chilly winter day
and, hungry, you can feast away!

My child, if you accept my words and treasure up my commandments within you...then you will understand the fear of the LORD and find the knowledge of God.
—*Proverbs 2:1, 5*

DIG, DIG, DIG. Bushy-tailed squirrels gather acorns all fall. Then, one by one, they bury them underground. This is how they store up food for winter. Those acorns will nourish them when times are tough. In the Bible, God also encourages us to store up things—not underground, but in our hearts! We don't need to store up acorns, but we can store up God's Word! How do we do this? We read the Bible and memorize special verses. Then, during hard times, just like squirrels with their acorns, we can be strengthened by God's messages of hope.

HEART MOMENT: Pick a few favorite verses from the Bible. Copy each verse onto a card. Then, like squirrels, "store" those cards in the nooks and crannies of your house so you can find and read them each day and be nourished. After a few times, you will have God's words memorized!

PETTING FARM

JOHN 10:11

One sheep, **two** goats, **three** squawking hens,
four horses neighing in their pens,
five little piglets run and squeal,
all ready for their evening meal.
I grab a pail with Farmer Fred
and we make sure they are well fed.

Jesus said to him, "Feed my lambs."

—John 21:15

BA-AH, OINK, NEIGH! Jesus wasn't a farmer at a petting zoo, but He does describe Himself as a Good Shepherd. A good shepherd cares for, feeds, and protects his sheep, even if it means risking his own life. Jesus does all this for us—including dying on the cross for our sins! And how do we show Him our thanks and love? Jesus said it best—by feeding His sheep! We feed His sheep by helping those in need and loving others in ways big and small.

HEART MOMENT: Make little sheep out of cotton balls. Then pretend you are the shepherd. As you lead them around your house and pretend to feed them, thank Jesus for being our Good Shepherd.

MY SWEATER
MATTHEW 25:34–40

My mama knit this sweater
when I was barely two
with buttons and a cozy hood
so woolly, soft, and blue.

Now that it's too small for me,
I wonder—what to do?
I'll wrap it with a pretty bow
and pass it on to you.

Do not neglect to do good and to share what you have, for such sacrifices are pleasing to God.

—*Hebrews 13:16*

HEAR YE, HEAR YE. Jesus told a story about a king.

"Welcome to my kingdom," the king said. "When I was in need, you fed and clothed me and cared for me."

But the king's guests were confused.

"When did we help you?" they asked.

"You helped me when you helped others in need," replied the king.

Jesus is our King. He *loves* when we share God's blessings and goodness with others.

HEART MOMENT: With an adult's help, gather up items you have outgrown or things you don't play with anymore. Put them in a box and deliver them to someone in need.

SNAIL PLAN

PSALM 27:13–14

Little snail, you're on the go.
But, you are very, very slow.
Patient, steadfast—that's your plan.
Can you do it? Yes, you can!

"I know the plans I have for you," announces the LORD. "I want you to enjoy success. I do not plan to harm you. I will give you hope for the years to come."

—*Jeremiah 29:11, NIrV*

S-O-O-O S-L-O-W! Sometimes it feels like God is very slow. We want Him to act *now* and to answer every prayer *right away.* But sometimes the answer is "No" or "Not yet." God is teaching us patience. Patience means being able to wait and trust God's timing and plan. The snail will eventually reach its destination. And God will answer our prayers and finish all His good plans when He thinks it's time. We can count on Him.

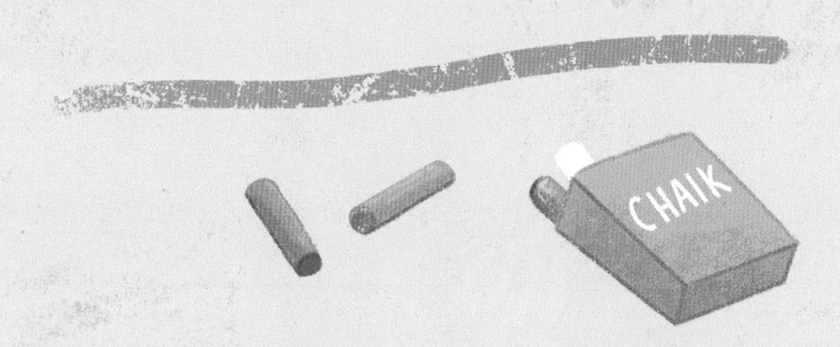

HEART MOMENT: Use chalk or string to mark a start and finish line on a sidewalk or lawn. Begin at the starting line and play a variation of "Simon Says" where you move forward in different ways but in slow motion. After your game, thank God that His timing is perfect.

FLUFFY STUFFY
1 JOHN 4:19

I have a fluffy stuffy,
I've had since I was born.
I bring it with me everywhere.
It's ragged, faded, worn.
It's oh-so-very huggable,
I love it to my core.
That's why it's so amazing that
God loves me even more!

...nor height, nor depth, nor anything else in all creation will be able to separate us from the love of God in Christ Jesus our Lord.

—Romans 8:39

HUG. HOLD. SQUEEZE. Do you have a special stuffed companion that you love with all your heart? Would you feel sad if you lost it? And would your love overflow even more when you found it? Well, here's an amazing thought: As much as you love your stuffy, God loves you even more! In fact, the reason we are able to love is because God first loved us! God's love is so deep and strong *nothing* can separate us from it. You might lose your stuffy, but you will never lose God's love.

HEART MOMENT: Find a special spot to snuggle with your stuffy. Tell it all the reasons you love it so much. Then, thank God for loving you for all those reasons and more!

BUILDING BLOCKS
GENESIS 11:1–9

Block by block, I build my fort
with wooden pieces, long and short.
Up, up it goes in solid rows
until, at last, on tippy toes,
when I cannot reach much higher,
I add the final, pointy spire.

Unless the Lord builds the house, those who build it labor in vain.

—Psalm 127:1

STACK, STACK, STACK. Long ago, God's people decided to build a tower. They pressed mud into blocks. "It will be the tallest tower in the world!" they cheered. "We'll be famous!" they chanted. But God was sad. In their excitement, they forgot about God. The people only thought about how smart they were and how well they could build. God wants us to build things and have fun, but in ways that honor Him and spread His love to others. He also wants us to include Him in our building plans because He is the Master Builder!

HEART MOMENT: Build something incredible out of blocks, then have a show-and-tell time. As you share what you have built, think of ways you can honor God and spread His love by using your talents to help others.

CHALK HEARTS
MARK 16:15

Pink hearts, green hearts, hearts with lines,
hearts with spots or fun designs.
I love drawing hearts with chalk
on my driveway, steps, and walk.
It's my artsy way to share
the love of Jesus everywhere!

Serve one another with whatever gift each of you has received.

—1 Peter 4:10

SCRITCH, SCRATCH, DRAW. Do you love to draw or make special things? Or to sing? Or to cook? God loves it when we use our gifts to spread His love. You can make a difference not just in your neighborhood but to the whole world! Before Jesus went back to heaven, He gave his followers a very important job. "Go into all the world and proclaim the good news." One way we do that is by sharing God's love using the gifts, or talents, God has given us!

HEART MOMENT: What are some of your special talents? Pick one. Then, think of a way you can use that talent to share God's love.

THE CROSS

1 JOHN 4:9–10

High upon a steeple,
or in a windowpane,
waving from a banner,
or hanging on a chain—

All around me, crosses,
each looking like a "t,"
remind me that King Jesus
died and rose again for me.

He himself bore our sins in his body on the cross, so that, having died to sins, we might live....

—1 Peter 2:24

HERE? THERE? Can you name three places you have seen crosses? Crosses remind us of God's greatest gift—a gift planned from the very beginning, when sin entered the world. Sin is doing wrong things. Sin hurts us because it separates us from God. So, what is the gift? The gift is Jesus, God's Son, who willingly died on the cross for our sins. But Jesus didn't stay dead. He rose again! If we put our trust in Jesus and accept His amazing gift of forgiveness and grace, we will live with Him forever too!

HEART MOMENT: Make your own "stained glass" cross on parchment or tracing paper. Begin by drawing the outline of a cross using a black marker. Next, add panes, also with black marker. Then color it and cut it out. Tape your "stained glass" cross in a sunny window as reminder of Jesus's greatest gift.

APPLE PICKING

LUKE 6:43–45

Let's run with our buckets in tow
to the orchard where, row after row,
sun-kissed apples abound,
plump and juicy and round
and perfect for picking to-go!

"Each tree is known by its own fruit."

—*Luke 6:44*

APPLES? PEACHES? What kind of fruit would you grow if you were a tree? A healthy tree gives plenty of fruit for others to enjoy. It's when there isn't any fruit that a farmer gets concerned. According to Scripture, people are like fruit trees. If we have Jesus in our hearts, we will produce good fruit for Him. But if we forget about Jesus and how much He loves it when we are kind and loving to others, we probably won't produce much good fruit for Him. Will you keep your heart healthy with God's love so you can produce good fruit?

HEART MOMENT: The next time you bite a crunchy apple or a juicy peach, list some ways you can produce good fruit for Jesus. Examples might include sharing your snack, saying "please" and "thank you," holding the door open for someone, putting away your toys, and more.

BATTER SPLATTER

PSALM 103:8

Standing on a kitchen chair,
I hold the bowl and mix with care.
Gently, now, or else—beware—
the batter splatters everywhere!

A gentle answer turns anger away. But mean words stir up anger.

—Proverbs 15:1, NIrV

STOMP. GRRRR. Have you ever felt mad? Instead of hugging your brother, you want to pull his hair or say something mean. You are like a kid with cake batter. You can either mix that batter gently and slowly to create a beautiful cake or whip it around and make a mess! Next time you feel angry or cranky, talk about it with a caring adult. Let God know, too, because He is slow to anger and full of love. If we ask, He will listen and help us work out our difficult emotions.

HEART MOMENT: Take some time today to share your feelings with a caring adult. Then, think of ways you can slow down, stay calm, and use gentle words with yourself and others.

HAMSTER HANDS
PSALM 145:14–18

I like to hold my hamster
and gently pet her head.
I cup my hands around her
like a cozy little bed.

I feel her small heart beating
as we talk about the day.
And when we both are ready
I put her down to play.

In his hand are the depths of the earth; the heights of the mountains are his also.

—Psalm 95:4

CUDDLE. CARE. As a boy, King David probably didn't have a pet hamster, but he had sheep! With gentle hands, David fed them, pulled them from danger, and carried them. No wonder David describes God's love as caring hands! In David's songs, called psalms, God holds us in His hands when we are afraid. He lifts us when we fall. He pours out blessings every day. God's hands are bigger than any human hands could ever be—so big that David tells us God's hands hold the whole world! An enormous God who loves every person on this planet—amazing!

HEART MOMENT: Imagine yourself being held in God's loving hands. Then sing the song "He's Got the Whole World in His Hands." Be sure to sing a verse with your name replacing "the whole world!"

SNOW CASTLE

MATTHEW 6:19–21

I made a castle out of snow
with towers and a room below.
The castle was my joy and pride,
with icy treasures tucked inside.
Then came spring—*drip, drip*—oh no!
It disappeared. Where did it go?

"Store up for yourselves treasures in heaven."

—*Matthew 6:20*

BRRR, COLD! Don't you wish snow or ice treasures could last forever? But what happens? They melt. And what happens to other treasures like favorite toys or trinkets? They get old and lose their shine. Soon they are no longer new. In fact, the only treasures that last forever, according to Jesus, are treasures from heaven. These include things like God's love, forgiveness, kindness, and eternal life in Jesus. Will you thank God today for these treasures from heaven?

HEART MOMENT: Find something that you treasure and give it a hug. Then give thanks that the treasures from heaven—like God's love—are even better than our most precious possessions.

BALLOON JOY

ACTS 2:38–39

Balloons at my party,
each held by a thread:
One purple, **two** yellow,
three orange, **four** red.
Now pumped full of air,
they bounce and they sway,
a wonderful, welcoming
birthday bouquet!

May the God of hope fill you with all joy and peace in believing, so that you may abound in hope by the power of the Holy Spirit.

—*Romans 15:13*

BOUNCE. BOP. SWAY. Filled with air, balloons joyfully welcome guests to a party. Did you know we are kind of like balloons? We aren't filled with air, but the Bible says when we accept Jesus as Lord, we are filled with the Holy Spirit. The Holy Spirit is our helper, filling us with hope, joy, understanding, and strength so we can follow God's ways. The Spirit also helps us when we pray. Will you welcome guests and spread God's love as you are filled with the Spirit?

HEART MOMENT: Using balloons or air-filled balls, gather in a circle and toss them around. As you play, give thanks that just as balloons or balls are pumped with air, God fills us with His Holy Spirit.

HEART DOOR

ROMANS 10:9–11

Some doors have windows. Some do not.
Some have screens for when it's hot.
Some roll up, while others slide.
Some have hinges on the side.
Some have a handle or a knob,
but *all* doors have a special job:
Tall or short or thick or thin,
doors are used to let guests in!

"Listen! I am standing at the door, knocking; if you hear my voice and open the door, I will come in."

—*Revelation 3:20*

KNOCK, KNOCK. Pretend your best friend is at the door. What do you do? Let him or her in. Then you spend the day doing special things together. In the Bible, Jesus describes Himself as standing at the door to our hearts, knocking. "Open the door," Jesus says, "so I can come in!" But Jesus is no ordinary guest. He's the most special guest ever! Jesus is our Savior, and He wants us to answer so He can love and guide us and be with us always!

HEART MOMENT: Color a large heart on a piece of paper. Then using old magazines and newspapers, look for pictures of doors. Cut them out and glue them onto the heart. As you do, give thanks that Jesus is knocking at the door to your heart. Will you let Him in?

INDEX

You may also be interested in these books by Laura Sassi and Sandra Eide...

My Tender Heart Bible
ISBN: 978-1-64060-839-9

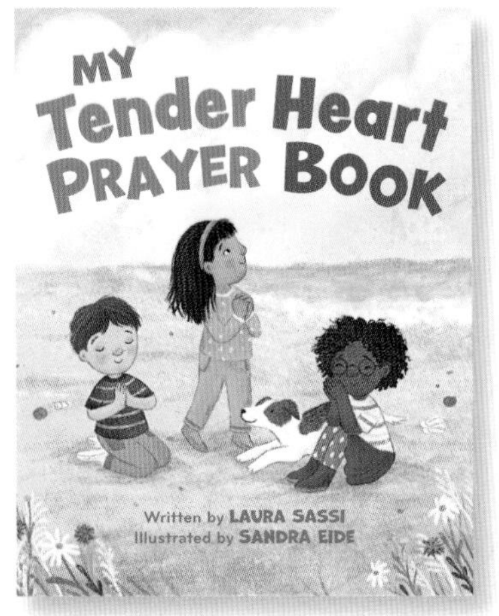

My Tender Heart Prayer Book
ISBN: 978-1-64060-842-9